UNCOVERING THE
ANALYZING PRIMARY SOURCES

WOMEN'S SU

Lynn Peppas

Crabtree Publishing Company
www.crabtreebooks.com

Author: Lynn Peppas
Editor-in-Chief: Lionel Bender
Editor: Simon Adams
Proofreader: Laura Booth,
 Wendy Scavuzzo
Project coordinator: Kelly Spence
Design and photo research: Ben White
Production: Kim Richardson
Production coordinator and
 prepress technician: Ken Wright
Print coordinator: Margaret Amy Salter

Consultant: Amie Wright,
The New York Public Library

This book was produced for
Crabtree Publishing Company by
Bender Richardson White

Photographs and reproductions:
Dreamstime: 38 Mid Rt (Creativei); 40 Mid (Agoes Rudianto). Getty Images: 39 Mid (Getty Images). Library and Archives of Canada: 28 Btm (e010933411-v8); 31 Btm Lft (Eugene M. Finn/National Film Board of Canada. Phototheque/PA-195432). Library of Congress: 1 Mid (LC-USZ62-30742); 3 Btm Mid (LC-USZ62-34032); 4 Top Lft (LC-USZ62-64309); 6 Top Rt (LC-DIG-ppmsca-02951); 8 Top Lft (LC-USZ62-130803); 11 Top Rt (LC-USZC4-4862); 14 Top Lft (LC-USZ62-28195); 14–15 Large (LC-DIG-ppmsca-02966); 17 Large (LC-DIG-ppmsca-02943); 18 Btm (LC-USZ62-135681); 19 Mid Rt (LC-DIG-ppmsca-08978); 23 Mid Rt (LC-DIG-ppmsca-02970); 24 Btm Rt (LC-USZ62-5535); 26–27 Mid (LC-USZ62-111143); 27 Mid Rt (LC-USZC4-1419); 29 Top Rt (LC-USZC4-9932); 30 Mid Lft (LC-DIG-ppmsca-02919); 32–033 Large (LC-DIG-ppmsca-26255); 35 Mid Rt (LC-USZ62-25338); 35 Btm (LC-DIG-ds-01453); 36 Top Lft (LC-DIG-ppmsc-01267). Rex Images: 36–37 Large (Rex Images). Shutterstock: 1 Full Page (Petrov Stanislav); 9 Mid Rt (Zack Frank); 13 Mid Rt (tristan tan); 13 Btm Rt (TinaImages); 32 Top Lft (Everett Historical); 34 Mid Lft (Everett Historical); 41 Btm (Anton Bielousov). Topfoto: 4–5 Large, 7 Btm Rt, 8–9 Mid, 10 Btm Rt, 12 Large (The Granger Collection); 16 Mid Rt (Topham/Photri); 20–21, 22 Btm, 25 Top, 29 Mid Lft (The Granger Collection).

Map: Stefan Chabluk
Cover photo: Library of Congress: Inez Mullholland
Photo shows suffragist and lawyer Inez Milholland Boissevain (1886-1916) at a women's suffrage parade in New York City, May 3, 1913.

Library and Archives Canada Cataloguing in Publication

Peppas, Lynn, author
 Women's suffrage / Lynn Peppas.

(Uncovering the past: analyzing primary sources)
Includes bibliographical references and index.
Issued in print and electronic formats.
ISBN 978-0-7787-1720-1 (bound).--
ISBN 978-0-7787-1722-5 (paperback).--
ISBN 978-1-4271-1683-3 (pdf).--ISBN 978-1-4271-1681-9 (html)

 1. Women--Suffrage--History--Juvenile literature. 2. Women--Suffrage--History--Sources--Juvenile literature. I. Title.

JF851.P47 2015   j324.6'23   C2015-903379-9
                                            C2015-903380-2

Library of Congress Cataloging-in-Publication Data

Peppas, Lynn.
 Women's suffrage / Lynn Peppas.
  pages cm -- (Uncovering the past: analyzing primary sources)
 Includes bibliographical references and index.
 ISBN 978-0-7787-1720-1 (reinforced library binding) --
ISBN 978-0-7787-1722-5 (pbk.) --
ISBN 978-1-4271-1683-3 (electronic pdf) --
ISBN 978-1-4271-1681-9 (electronic html)
1. Women--Suffrage--History--Sources--Juvenile literature. 2. Women--Suffrage--History--Juvenile literature. 3. Suffragists--History--Juvenile literature. I. Title.

JF851.P47 2016
324.6'23--dc23
                                            2015019711

Crabtree Publishing Company

Printed in Canada/082015/BF20150630

www.crabtreebooks.com   1-800-387-7650

Copyright © **2016 CRABTREE PUBLISHING COMPANY.** All rights reserved. No part of this publication may be reproduced, stored in a retrieval system or be transmitted in any form or by any means, electronic, mechanical, photocopying, ecording, or otherwise, without the prior written permission of Crabtree Publishing Company. In Canada: We acknowledge the financial support of the Government of Canada through the Canada Book Fund for our publishing activities.

Published in Canada	**Published in the United States**	**Published in the United Kingdom**	**Published in Australia**
Crabtree Publishing	Crabtree Publishing	Crabtree Publishing	Crabtree Publishing
616 Welland Ave.	PMB 59051	Maritime House	3 Charles Street
St. Catharines, ON	350 Fifth Avenue, 59th Floor	Basin Road North, Hove	Coburg North
L2M 5V6	New York, NY 10118	BN41 1WR	VIC, 3058

UNCOVERING THE PAST

REMEMBERING THE PAST

"People must know the past to understand the present and to face the future."

Canadian suffragist leader, Nellie McClung, 1945

The past is everything that has happened up to this moment in time, but the past is impossible to know. The only way to truly know about an event or time is if you have lived it. Although **history** tells us about the past, it is never the complete story. History is a written record of a particular time or event. History gives us a small glimpse into the past. Even **historians** cannot know everything that once happened.

Historians learn about an event or era by examining the pieces of **evidence**—called **primary sources**—that have been preserved. Historians have a lot in common with detectives. Both **analyze** evidence to determine what really happened. Historians evaluate and interpret **primary sources** to help them understand as much as they can about the past. Interpreting primary sources is not easy. Often we think we know about a subject from listening to others, watching television, or reading books. But not everything we read, see, or hear is always true. We look at primary sources to form our own understanding of what happened.

DEFINITIONS

We can define historical time in different ways:

A **decade** is a period of ten years, a **century** 100 years, and a **millennium** 1,000 years. A **generation** is all the people born and living at the same time such as Generation X (1960–1980).

An **era** is a period of time with a certain characteristic, such as the Roaring Twenties (the 1920s). An **age** is a long period of time, such as the Stone Age.

◀ In 1913, **suffragists** marched up Fifth Avenue in New York to demand the **vote.**

WOMEN'S RIGHTS: AN OVERVIEW

The struggle for women to be accepted as equals in society has been a long journey. In many **cultures** throughout history, women were controlled first by their fathers and later by their husbands. Laws formed to protect people often did not apply to women. Women were the property of men and often had only a few more rights than **slaves**.

This **inequality** continued for North American women as late as the 1900s. Women were not allowed to further their education in

Publish'd at Philad.ª Dec.ʳ 1.ˢᵗ 1792.

DEFINITIONS

The terms used to describe people often change over time:

Aboriginal: A term used to describe people whose ancestors were the original inhabitants of a country

African American: Americans whose ancestors came from Africa

Black: Another term for African Americans

Fair sex: An old-fashioned term used for a person of the female gender or sex; the word fair was associated with beauty

First Nations: A term used to describe some of the aboriginal people living in Canada, although it does not include the Inuit people, who are also aboriginal

ANALYZE THIS

The Lady's Magazine: or Entertaining Companion for the Fair Sex was first published in the United Kingdom in 1770. Who are the "Fair Sex?" Even though it is a magazine for women, and considering that most of the writers and editors of the magazine were male, what might this source tell you about women in the late 1700s?

> *"Again, the male is by nature superior, and the female inferior; and the one rules, and the other is ruled; this principle, of necessity, extends to all mankind."*
>
> Aristotle, *Politics*, 350 BCE

colleges and universities. Most men believed that women's intellect was inferior to that of men's. Women were not allowed to practice medicine or law. Married women could not own property. Everything they had legally belonged to their husband. In a divorce, the children were awarded to the father.

Women could do little to change these laws because they were not allowed to vote. In fact, it has only been in about the last 100 years that some women in North America have been allowed to vote. For many others, such as aboriginal and black women, the right to vote has only been given in the last 50 years.

As a result of male-controlled societies throughout time, much of *his*tory from ancient times to about the 1800s has been written *by* men *for* men. *Her*story—the documentation of the past from a female perspective—is a new word **coined** in the 1970s by the **feminist** writer Robin Morgan. Women recording history from their point of view is a new event that has only occurred within the past 200 years.

◀ This illustration from the opening pages of a magazine called *The Lady's Magazine: or Entertaining Companion for the Fair Sex* shows Liberty with a copy of Mary Wollstonecraft's *A Vindication of the Rights of Woman.*

▶ In 1914, the British **suffragette** Emmeline Pankhurst was arrested for trying to give a petition to King George V demanding the vote.

ANALYZE THIS

By looking at the men's expressions in this photograph, what is their feeling over the situation? What does Mrs. Pankhurst's expression tell you?

TYPES OF EVIDENCE

"Let woman share the rights and she will [equal] the virtues of man; for she must grow more perfect when emancipated, or justify the authority that chains such a weak being to her duty."

Feminist writer Mary Wollstonecraft, from *A Vindication of the Rights of Woman*, 1792

A primary source is historical evidence created by a person who was involved in a particular event or time period. Primary sources give the best clues as to what really happened. They come in many different formats, including **artifacts**, **documents**, and personal accounts.

Artifacts are physical objects that were made or used during an event or era. Examples of artifacts associated with women's rights include items such as clothing, cooking **utensils**, and household appliances. Documents are records, usually on paper, that relate to a time or event. Examples of documents include a written **constitution** or law, a property or tax receipt, or a written play. Finally, a personal account is one person's memories of a time or event. A personal account includes a diary or journal entry, an interview for a newspaper or other **media** source, or simply talking to someone who witnessed an event.

In the not-too-distant past, most people handwrote their thoughts in journals or in mailed letters that have been preserved. The technology of how media is recorded, displayed, and preserved has drastically changed in the past 20 years. Many people today create information sources in electronic e-mails, texts, websites, smartphones with cameras, and **blogs**. These primary sources also serve as historical primary sources for the future.

National W

President, SUSAN B. ANTHONY,
Rochester, N. Y.
Ch'n Ex. Com. MATILDA JOSLYN GAGE,
Fayetteville, N. Y.
Cor. Sec'y, JANE GRAHAM JONES,
910 Prairie Ave., Chicago, Ill
For. Cor. Sec'y, LAURA CURTIS BULLARD,
56 East Thirty-ninth St., New York.
Rec. Sec'y, MARY F. DAVIS,
Orange, New Jersey
Treasurer, ELLEN C. SARGENT,
Washington, D. C.

and House of ... assembler,...

We the United States, ... and immuni... the right to vot... losing Resol... Resolved; Tha... of the National Convention ... Congress to en... during its pres... citizens in ... Union, in

▶ In 1878, the National Woman Suffrage Association (NWSA) petitioned Congress for the right to vote. The petition is signed by Susan B. Anthony and Elizabeth Cady Stanton.

Suffrage Association.

1873.

Honorable Senate
...entatives in Congress

...igned, citizens
...ived of some of
...tizens, ...
...leave to submit

...the officers and
...Suffrage Ass...
...ed; Respectf...
...propriate leg...
...tion to pro...
...everal State...
...right to vote,

...n B. Anthony Pr...
...ilda Joslyn Gage Ch. Ex. Com.
...h Cady Stanton

ANALYZE THIS

This letter is a preserved written record and primary source of the struggle for women's **suffrage.** Who created this document? When was it written? Who was it written to? Do you believe this to be a **reliable** primary source? Why or why not?

Are these bronze sculptures (below) primary sources? Why, or why not?

▲ The *First Wave* sculpture features life-sized bronze figures of the five women who organized the first women's rights **convention** in North America in 1848, as well as a few of the men who came to support them. The sculptures were created by American artist Lloyd Lillie and his assistants in the 1990s.

SECONDARY SOURCES

A **secondary source** is a person's interpretation of a historical event or time period. A person who produces a secondary source did not actually witness or participate in the event or era. Artists, writers, historians, and other people sometimes recreate historical descriptions by investigating, interpreting, and evaluating the existing primary sources.

An **online** newspaper article about a bank robbery would be a secondary source, unless the reporter was at the bank during the **heist**. But if the reporter interviewed and included the **eyewitness** accounts of people present at the heist in their article, the actual quotes are

ANALYZE THIS

Looking at the cover page of this song **score**, why do you think the composer wrote this song? Why is the song written for "Mrs. J. M. Ashley?" Are the lyrics from a song published in 1869 considered a primary or secondary source? Why?

▶ This is the cover page for the score of the song "We'll Show You When We Come to Vote," written by American composer Frank Howard in 1869.

TYPES OF SECONDARY SOURCES

Secondary sources have used one or more primary sources to form opinions or reach conclusions. They have collected evidence and interpreted it for you already. Secondary sources include:

- Textbooks
- Newspaper or magazine articles about an event in the past
- Websites
- Historical paintings
- Historically based movies and documentaries
- Maps created today to show historical information
- Interview of an expert on a topic, unless the person directly experienced a topic or event

▲ Louise Hall and Susan Fitzgerald pasted billboard posters about women's suffrage in Cincinnati in May 1912.

primary sources even though the article is still a secondary source. To determine if a source is primary or secondary, always ask yourself: "Was the person creating it present?"

Secondary sources are not as reliable as primary sources. It is impossible to know precisely what happened in the past because not every moment of an event has been recorded. A secondary source can only be as good as the primary sources that the historian has analyzed to determine their version of history.

"Sad is the life of womankind,
Tred under foot we've always been,
But when we vote, you soon will find
That we'll fix these "terrible men.""

Chorus from the song, "We'll Show You When We Come to Vote," by Frank Howard, 1869

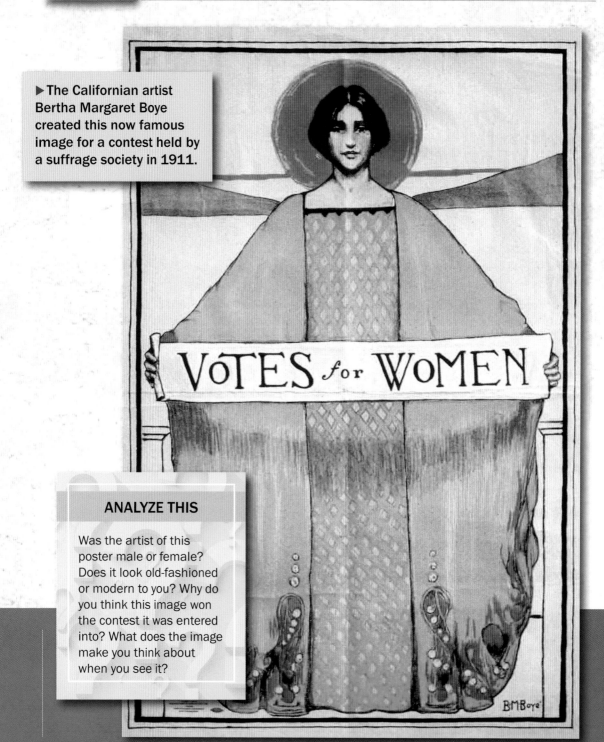

▶ The Californian artist Bertha Margaret Boye created this now famous image for a contest held by a suffrage society in 1911.

VOTES for WOMEN

ANALYZE THIS

Was the artist of this poster male or female? Does it look old-fashioned or modern to you? Why do you think this image won the contest it was entered into? What does the image make you think about when you see it?

FINDING RELIABLE SOURCES

Some primary sources are considered better than others. For example, an eyewitness who gives their account of what happened directly after an event occurs is considered more reliable than even that same person's account of the same event 20 years later.

A primary source is also more reliable when a different source supports the evidence it gives. For example, if you read one woman's diary entry about a women's rights meeting she attended, it becomes even more **credible** if you can also find a newspaper article or photograph that gives similar evidence of the same meeting.

A secondary source is much like a primary source in that the ones created closer to the time or event are considered to be more reliable than ones created many years later. But a secondary source is, at best, someone else's interpretation of history. It is almost always more rewarding to see and learn from the evidence firsthand.

PHOTOGRAPHS

Photographs became widely used by 1839 to record images. Until the late 1800s, a subject had to be very still for up to 30 seconds to produce a clear image. Having one's photograph taken was a serious occasion: Most people did not own cameras and it certainly was not like today's multiple and daily selfies. It wasn't until about 1919 that photographs were regularly used in North American newspapers and magazines. Most were produced in black and white until about 1960. After that time, color images were easier to produce.

"*A woman is nobody. A wife is everything. A pretty girl is equal to ten thousand men, and a mother is, next to God, all powerful . . .*"

Extract from the *Public Ledger and Daily Transcript*, published in Philadelphia in 1881

▲ The stamp at the top celebrates the 50th anniversary of women's suffrage in 1970. The lower stamp celebrates Rosie the Riveter, an American national symbol of women workers during World War II.

INTERPRETATION

"I had never before heard a woman speak at a public meeting. She said but a few words, but these were spoken so modestly . . . She apologized for what might be regarded as an intrusion, but was assured . . . that what she had said was very acceptable."

J. Miller McKim writing about hearing Lucretia Mott speak at an American Anti-Slavery Society meeting in 1833

Every primary source is created for a specific reason. It is your job to analyze a source by asking yourself basic questions to learn more about why it was created and what it means historically. This process is called **sourcing** and it involves asking questions about a primary source:

- What is the source?
- Who created it?
- Why was this source created?
- Where was this source created?
- What does the source prove, claim, show, or say?
- What else was going on around the same time?

   Consider the **quotation** given here by J. Miller McKim. This account was written after a meeting held in Philadelphia in 1833. We don't know exactly why or who McKim originally created it for, but sometimes primary sources don't give all the answers you're looking for. McKim was evidently impressed by the fact that a woman spoke so **eloquently** at a public meeting. His account gives a clue as how men may have thought about women and their public-speaking abilities. Mott's "apology" and "modesty" that McKim wrote about is another possible clue that Mott may have felt uncomfortable speaking in a public setting.

▲ These two pages from the scrapbooks of Elizabeth Smith Miller and Anne Fitzhugh Miller display a photograph, brochures, press clippings, and other items related to the Men's League for Woman Suffrage and the Equal Franchise Society.

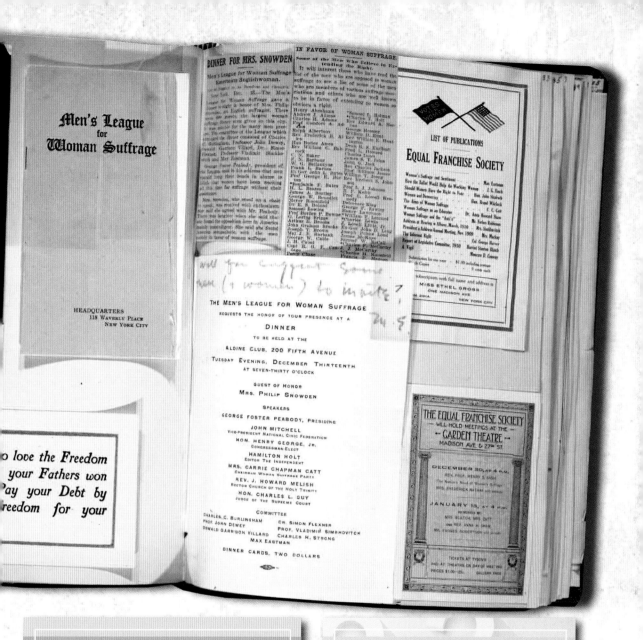

PERSPECTIVES

Men actively supported women's suffrage, too. These scrapbook pages contain multiple documents related to the Men's League for Woman Suffrage and the Equal Franchise Society. The league was formed in about 1910 and had about 20,000 members by 1912.

FINDING CONTEXT

Further research—or finding **context**—of people's cultural attitudes during that time will help you interpret this primary source to a greater degree. If you knew more information, such as that Lucretia Mott was a Quaker minister, and that she and her husband James Mott were active and well-known **abolitionists**, would that change your interpretation of the source?

You may conclude that Mott would be comfortable talking to a large group of people, considering that she was a minister. Do you think most American men in 1833 felt the same way as McKim about Mott's speech? Now that you know more about the people discussed in this primary source, read the quotation again. How does finding out context change your ideas about the clues to be found in this primary source?

Almost all sources—primary or secondary—are created with some degree of **bias**. Bias is the outlook, or personal opinions, that a person has. Everyone is biased is some way in how they think, write, create, and even talk to others. A person's cultural upbringing, the television shows they watch, their teachers, the music they enjoy, the books and newspapers they read, all shape a person's personal bias. In turn, when a person creates a primary or secondary source, they bring their own personal bias to the evidence. Bias is not a bad thing and it does not make a source unreliable. But when analyzing a primary or secondary source, you must consider the creator's bias and how it affects the meaning.

▲ This painting depicts Susan B. Anthony (1820–1906), who played a major role in the American women's suffrage movement. Her work led to American women getting the vote in 1920.

"The curtain now we'll kindly draw, O'er this sad scene of strife
A husband who has put his foot, Right down upon his wife.
It's very sad she was so bad, Dear Husbands, take example,
And if you get a suffragette, Just make this play your sample."

Epilogue from the play *The Militant Husbandette*, produced in Des Moines, Iowa, in 1913

◄ *Life* magazine on February 20, 1913, showed a Susan B. Anthony-like person in classical dress thrusting her rolled umbrella at a man wearing a toga. The issue is described as the "Husbandette's Number."

ANALYZE THIS

Observe the top left-hand corner of this cover of *Life* magazine. What was the meaning of "**husbandette**" in 1913? To what do you think it is referring? What does the style of the cover art remind you of? Why do you think the artist chose this style?

GETTING TO THE TRUTH

A primary source's evidence is more reliable when it is supported by similar information from one or more independent primary sources. Take, for example, the abolitionist and women's rights **activist** Sojourner Truth's famous speech, "Ain't I A Woman?" given during the Women's Rights Convention in Akron, Ohio, in 1851.

There is no actual document of Truth's written speech because Truth could not read or write. But a few people present at the convention recreated parts of her speech. A newspaper article was published in the *Anti-Slavery Bugle* on June 21, 1851, a little less than a month after the actual speech. Here's a quote from the article about Truth's speech:

". . . I am a woman's rights. I have as much muscle as any man, and can do as much work as any man. I have plowed and reaped and husked and chopped and mowed, and can any man do more than that? I have heard much about the sexes being equal; I can carry as much as any man . . .

"As for intellect, all I can say is, if a woman have a pint and a man a quart— why can't she have her little pint full? You need not be afraid to give us our rights

▼ While the women on the floor of the hall discuss women's rights in 1859, the men are restricted to the balconies above.

Yᴱ MAY SESSION OF Yᴱ WOMAN'S RIGHTS CONVENTION—Yᴱ ORATOR OF Yᴱ DAY DENOUNCING Yᴱ LORDS OF CREATION.

HARPER'S WEEKLY.
[JUNE 11, 1859.

> ▶ **Sojourner Truth (c. 1797–1883)** was an anti-slavery campaigner and a women's rights activist.

I Sell the Shadow to Support the Substance.

SOJOURNER TRUTH.

for fear we will take too much—for we won't take more than our pint will hold."

The most famous version of "Ain't I A Woman?" was written down by the president of the convention, Frances Gage, in 1863, 12 years after the event:

". . . Then they talk about this thing in the head; what's this they call it? [member of audience whispers 'intellect'] That's it, honey. What's that got to do with women's rights or negroes' rights? If my cup won't hold but a pint, and yours holds a quart, wouldn't you be mean not to let me have my little half measure full?"

It is impossible to know exactly what Sojourner Truth said in her speech in 1851. But by comparing the two independent primary sources of the same event, do you see points made that are the same or different? What can you **infer** about Truth's speech given these two examples? Which of the two do you feel is more reliable?

"Look at me! Look at my arm! I have ploughed and planted, and gathered into barns, and no man could [do better than] me! And ain't I a woman?"

Excerpt from Sojourner Truth's famous speech given at the Women's Rights Convention in Akron, Ohio, 1851

HERSTORY

WOMEN'S SUFFRAGE

"Women have invaded many of the trades and some of the professions . . . We believe there has been no female lawyer, and probably will be none. The pen, many of the fine arts, they have made their own . . . as writers, as musicians, as painters, as actors . . . "

From *Woman in the Nineteenth Century* by Margaret Fuller Ossoli, 1845

In the 1830s, some women in North America were becoming active in social **reform** movements that were trying to change the long-held **social standards** by which everyone lived. Women organized **temperance** and abolition societies, the latter to fight for the freedom and rights of African Americans.

It was during the World Anti-Slavery Convention in London in 1840 that two American women, Elizabeth Cady Stanton and Lucretia Mott, were inspired to start a new movement. Mott and other women delegates to the conference were not allowed to participate because they were women. Afterward, Stanton and Mott spoke about forming a society to fight for women's rights.

Eight years later, Mott and Stanton organized the first American women's rights convention in Seneca Falls, New York. During the meeting, 68 women and 32 men, including the abolitionist Frederick Douglass, signed the Declaration of Sentiments — a document written by Stanton that closely imitated the American Declaration of Independence. Many were shocked when Stanton proposed suffrage for women, even Mott! But the declaration set the tone for future women's rights movements.

▶ The National Woman Suffrage Association was founded in 1869 by Susan B. Anthony and Elizabeth Cady Stanton, both shown here standing in front of the audience.

ANALYZE THIS

What in this engraving might suggest that the National Woman Suffrage Association was newly formed? By looking at the audience, did men or women typically attend these meetings? How did American women dress in the 1870s? Did they always dress like this or just for important meetings?

JOIN THE NATIONAL WOMAN'S SUFFRAGE ASSOCIATION

UNCOVERING THE PAST

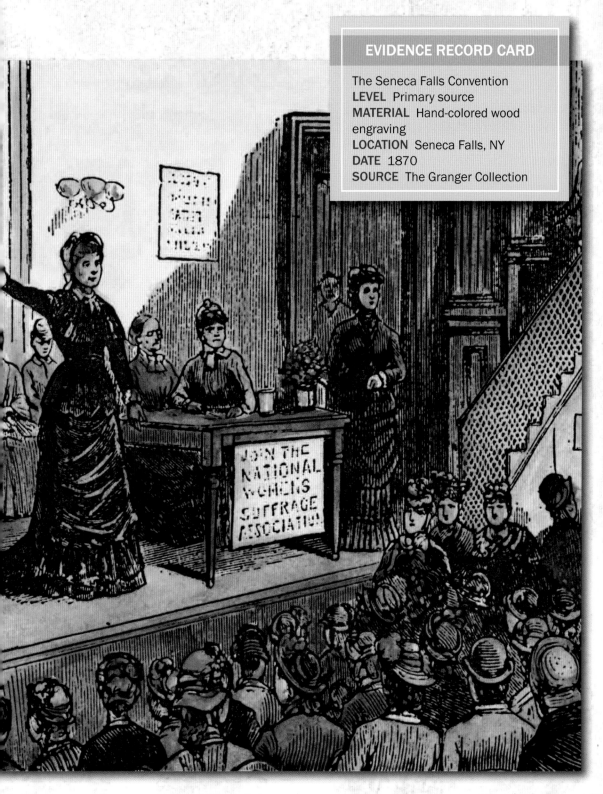

JOIN THE NATIONAL WOMENS SUFFRAGE ASSOCIATION

THE FIGHT CONTINUES

The American Civil War (1861–1865) **emancipated** African Americans. After the war, the women's rights movement gained even more momentum. In 1866, Elizabeth Cady Stanton and Susan B. Anthony founded the American Equal Rights Association (AERA) with a goal to get suffrage for all persons regardless of gender or race. The Fourteenth **Amendment**, **ratified** in 1868, allowed voting rights for every male citizen. While it was being drawn up, Stanton and Anthony fought to have the word "male" removed, but some feared the bill would not pass if women's suffrage were included.

Two national suffrage organizations were formed in the United States in 1869. Anthony and Stanton formed the National Woman Suffrage Association (NWSA). Lucy Stone, her husband Henry Blackwell, and Julia Ward Howe formed the American Woman Suffrage Association (AWSA). Each organization fought for women's suffrage in a different way.

The Fifteenth Amendment, ratified in 1870, gave all citizens regardless of race and color the right to vote, but still did not include women. During the

▼ **Victoria Claflin Woodhull read her argument in favor of women's suffrage before the Judiciary Committee of the House of Representatives in 1871. Directly behind her is Elizabeth Cady Stanton, with Susan B. Anthony at the far left.**

presidential election of 1872, Anthony and more than 100 other women tried to cast their vote. Many, such as Sojourner Truth, were turned away at the polls. But Anthony and a few others succeeded, and were arrested and fined. Virginia Minor, one of the suffragists who had tried to vote, took the matter to the Supreme Court in 1875 but lost her case. The **repercussion** of this loss meant that each individual state determined who could vote. Some Southern states passed laws that required African Americans to own land or take a test to be able to register to vote.

PERSPECTIVES

What type of bias would you expect to find in a suffragist-sponsored newspaper? Would you find the same bias in a report of the same event found in a newspaper such as *The New York Times* or *Washington Post*? What do you think might be different or the same?

▼ Suffragist newspapers, such as *Woman's Journal*, published through the AWSA, and *The Revolution*, published through the NWSA, educated their readers on women's rights issues such as suffrage, discrimination, divorce, and domestic violence.

"The history of mankind is a history of repeated injuries and usurpations on the part of man toward woman, having in direct object the establishment of an absolute tyranny over her."

From the Declaration of Sentiments, a document written by Elizabeth Cady Stanton in 1848

SLOW PROGRESS

Senator Aaron Sargent introduced to Congress in 1878 the Woman Suffrage Amendment—also known as the Susan B. Anthony Amendment, due to Anthony's work in drafting the bill. But the bill was not passed. Suffragists began to work toward gaining suffrage through state governments instead of amending the national constitution. In 1890, the NWSA and AWSA combined to become one organization called the National American Woman Suffrage Association (NAWSA).

Some American women first gained their right to vote in Wyoming Territory in 1869. By 1912, more western states—Colorado, Utah, Idaho, Washington, California, Michigan, Kansas, Oregon, Territory of Alaska, and Arizona—had also **enfranchised** women. But many states, mainly to the south and northeast of the country, did not allow female suffrage.

CANADIAN WOMEN

Emily Howard Stowe pioneered the women's rights movement in Canada. Stowe applied to two Ontario colleges in 1852 and 1865, but was refused admission both times because she was a woman.

Stowe moved to New York in 1867 and earned her medical degree at the New York Medical College for Women. She then moved back to Toronto and became the first woman physician to practice in Canada. Her education struggles inspired her to found Canada's first suffrage organization, known as the

▶ The American **lithographer** Louis Prang produced this image of seven *Representative Women* in 1870. Photographers did not have the technology we enjoy today and the production was very complex.

◀ To get the attention of their nations and to further their cause, women's suffrage groups organized parades, wrote and produced plays, and **picketed**.

Toronto Women's Literary Guild, in 1877. In 1883, it was renamed the Canadian Women's Suffrage Association.

Women in Canada faced similar national reactions to suffrage. In 1883, Canada's prime minister John A. MacDonald introduced a bill to parliament that would grant suffrage to some women, but it was defeated two years in a row.

The National Council of Women of Canada, formed in 1884, fought for women's rights and suffrage. Canadian women slowly gained suffrage at a **municipal** level, but it was not for all women. In most provinces, it was for unmarried women or widows only. In the 1890s, bills for women's suffrage were introduced but all were defeated. Some Canadian women gained partial suffrage through their **provincial government**. Manitoba was the first province to enfranchise women at a provincial level on January 27, 1916.

"While the Nation is buoyant with patriotism . . . on this hundredth anniversary of our country's birth . . . we cannot forget, even in this glad hour, that while all men of every race, and [climate], and condition, have been invested with the full rights of citizenship, under our hospitable flag, all women still suffer the degradation of dis[en]franchisement."

An excerpt from the "Declaration of Rights of the Women of the United States," written by Stanton and Anthony for the NWSA on the centennial celebration of the Declaration of Independence, July 4, 1876

WORLD WAR I

Canada entered World War I in 1914 and the United States followed later in 1917. As millions of men in North America left their jobs to fight in the war, women filled the gaps they left in the workforce. Some women joined in the war effort as **stenographers** and nurses. Others did nontraditional jobs such as working at munitions, or weapons, factories. Women's contributions did not go unnoticed and helped change how many men felt about women's suffrage.

In Canada, the 1917 Wartime Elections Act enfranchised the wives, mothers, and sisters of soldiers for federal (national) elections. That included any woman in the military or working overseas as a nurse during World War I. It was the first step toward achieving full women's suffrage in Canada.

U.S. President Woodrow Wilson was against women's suffrage in 1913 when he first entered office. But the issue became harder to ignore during women's patriotic involvement in the war effort. In 1917, some women picketers, including suffragist leader Alice Paul, were unjustly arrested and jailed for picketing. Some of those arrested went on a **hunger strike** to protest their illegal imprisonment, and were force-fed by prison guards. On November 14, 1917, prison guards beat more than 30 imprisoned women suffragists. The event gained the attention and sympathy of many Americans, including President Wilson. Two months later, on January 10, 1918, the House of Representatives passed the Woman Suffrage Amendment. It was on its way to becoming law.

"We have made partners of the women in this war; shall we admit them only to a partnership of suffering and sacrifice and toil and not to a partnership of privilege and right?"

U.S. President Woodrow Wilson's appeal to the Senate to ratify the Woman Suffrage Amendment, September 30, 1918

▼ The General Federation of Women's
Clubs (GFWC) worked with the Young
Men's Christian Association (YMCA) to
send about 100 women overseas to help
wounded soldiers after World War I.

FOR EVERY FIGHTER
A WOMAN WORKER

Y·W·C·A·

BACK OUR SECOND LINE OF DEFENSE
UNITED WAR WORK CAMPAIGN

▲ During World War I,
women took over many jobs
previously done by men,
including welding car parts.

SUCCESS AT LAST!

Canadian women were first federally enfranchised in 1918. Female citizens who could vote had to be: "Age 21 or older, not **alien-born** and meet property requirements in provinces where they exist." To qualify for provincial suffrage, some provinces required women to own property to vote. In 1920, the Dominion Elections Act was passed that enfranchised most women, regardless of provincial laws.

In the United States, Congress approved the Nineteenth Amendment in 1919. It was ratified on

ANALYZE THIS

Notice how these women ambulance drivers are dressed. Looking back at earlier photos of how women suffragists dressed, what women's clothing articles drastically changed from this photograph? Could women ambulance drivers repair car engines or tires and do their work as easily if they dressed in earlier female fashions?

▼ Alice Isaacson owned this photograph of "The Motor Ambulance A-1 Girls." She was an American nurse who served with the Canadian Forces in World War I.

August 26, 1920, and amended to the constitution of the United States. This promised that the "right of citizens of the United States to vote shall not be denied or abridged by the United States or by any State on account of sex." It had taken American suffrage activists 72 years to win the fight.

Even though many women were enfranchised by 1920, not all North American women could vote. It would take further activism and many more decades for women of all races to have the right to vote.

◀ Many women wore badges, such as this, advocating votes for women.

▲ During World War I, many women did invaluable war-work as shorthand typists while the men fought in the war.

"If women had the vote there would be no need to come twice asking for better legislation for women and children, no need to come again and again for the appointment of women inspectors where women and children are employed; we would not ask in vain for the raising of the wage or consent."

Canadian suffragist Henrietta Muir Edwards, speaking at the Women's Christian Temperance Union's Convention, October 1907

THE FIGHT CONTINUES

In the early 1900s, the NAWSA introduced the idea that only "educated women" should be allowed to vote. This excluded many African-American women who could not afford an education due to circumstances beyond their control. Some states, especially in the South, passed laws that **disenfranchised** women based on race.

Fannie Lou Hamer fought for African–American suffrage so that black women

◀ This cartoon entitled "The Sky is Now Her Limit" was published in 1920 in *The New York Times*. Each rung on the ladder stands for the condition of women in society. As the woman climbs upward—toward the top rung marked "Presidency"—the rungs show better opportunities for women.

ANALYZE THIS

Looking at this cartoon, do you think the illustrator would have been surprised by the fact that in 2016, a woman had not yet been elected as president of the United States?

"To this end, Congress should enact a law for 'educated suffrage' for our native born as well as foreign rulers, alike ignorant of our institutions. With free schools and compulsory education no one has an excuse for not understanding the language of the country."
Elizabeth Cady Stanton, speaking at the NAWSA convention, February 12–18, 1902

could improve their lives by voting for politicians who supported them. She was from Mississippi, where African Americans had to pass a test to register to vote. In 1962, she was fired from her job for trying to register to vote. In 1963, she and others involved in a voter registration workshop were unjustly arrested and beaten by Mississippi state patrol officers. During the Democratic National Convention in Atlantic City, New Jersey, on August 22, 1964, she made a publically televised speech about her treatment at that time.

The same year Hamer co-founded the Mississippi Freedom Democratic Party. Her powerful testimony furthered the civil rights and suffrage movements. Almost one year later, President Johnson signed the Voting Rights Act of 1965 into law. This meant that a person could not be denied suffrage in the United States because of their race.

Some women in Canada, too, were not allowed to vote because of their race, such as aboriginal or Japanese-Canadian women. Japanese Canadians—male or female—living in British Columbia were not enfranchised until 1948. Aboriginal Canadians—First Nations, Métis, and Inuit peoples—had to give up their **Indian status** to be enfranchised. Giving up one's Indian status meant that an aboriginal person lost their cultural identity, could not live in a reserve community, and did not enjoy the benefits of treaties and laws for Canadian aboriginal peoples. All aboriginal women and men—no matter what their status—were given full suffrage in Canada in 1960.

▼ The "Famous 5" women, plus a male supporter, who gained the right for all Canadian women to be considered as "persons" by law.

THE ARGUMENTS AGAINST

"Young man, if you don't want a female lawyer, doctor or politician for a wife, but would prefer a woman who will be a good companion, home maker, wife and mother, [then] vote and induce all your friends to vote against EQUAL SUFFRAGE."

"Anti-Woman Suffrage: Don't Fail to Read This" leaflet distributed in Denver, Colorado, 1893

Not everyone believed that women should have equal rights and suffrage. In the late 1800s and early 1900s, some people were strongly opposed to change. The movement was called anti-suffragism. Anti-suffragists—"antis"—were mostly women. They believed that suffrage would not make their lives better and might make matters worse. Among the arguments against women's suffrage were:

- Women are not as intelligent as men and are more emotional and could not make good political decisions.
- Politics would **corrupt** a woman's mind.
- Men would be less **chivalrous** toward women.
- A woman's realm was the household and family life; a man's was in business and politics.
- If women got the vote, they may not marry and have children, and the human race would die out.
- Women do not fight in wars for their country and therefore shouldn't get the vote.
- Most women are not interested in politics or suffrage.
- The electoral system has never included women before and has worked well; why change it now?
- If women got the vote, the next step would be for them to become politicians.
- Women are already represented by their male relatives. If a woman voted with her husband, it would double his vote, if she voted against him it would cancel it out.
- Women would compete against men instead of cooperating with them.
- Women's suffrage would increase election expenses.

▲ In *Why Not Go the Limit?* by artist Harry Grant Dart, published in 1908, women are shown smoking and drinking in a bar.

▶ Poking fun at suffragettes, this card states that "Everybody works but mother, she's a suffragette."

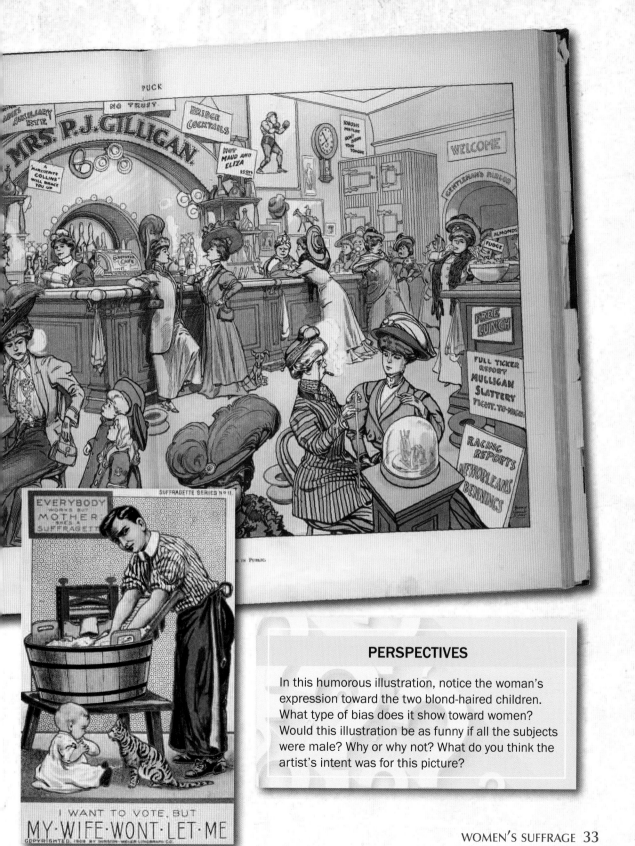

PERSPECTIVES

In this humorous illustration, notice the woman's expression toward the two blond-haired children. What type of bias does it show toward women? Would this illustration be as funny if all the subjects were male? Why or why not? What do you think the artist's intent was for this picture?

ANTI-SUFFRAGISM

The New York State Association Opposed to Woman Suffrage was first organized in 1897. The all-female members believed that enfranchisement went against the laws of nature, and that a woman's place was at home caring for the household and having a family.

The organization published numerous pamphlets, explaining their opposition to women's suffrage. In 1908, one of the members, Mrs. William Winslow Crannell, began publishing a **quarterly** magazine called *The Anti-Suffragist*. The magazine published articles about women who did not want suffrage, and reported on suffrage groups that had failed in their protests. It also published examples of those western states that had enfranchised women, but argued that

▼ This anti-women's suffrage poster was produced in California in October 1911. California eventually passed suffrage laws for women in 1912.

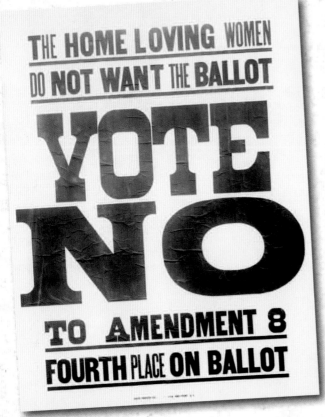

THE HOME LOVING WOMEN DO NOT WANT THE BALLOT

VOTE NO

TO AMENDMENT 8 FOURTH PLACE ON BALLOT

PERSPECTIVES

Who was this poster created for: men or women? How are the women who "do not want the **ballot**" described as being? How would "antis" want you to think about women who do want the ballot? Do you think women who supported suffrage could be home-loving women, too?

"Housewives! You do not need a ballot to clean out your sink spout. A handful of potash and some boiling water is quicker and cheaper."
Household hints pamphlet, published by the National Association Opposed to Woman Suffrage, in 1910

their votes had not made society better. The magazine continued until April 1912.

In 1911, the New York organization joined with other state anti-suffrage groups whose women had not yet been enfranchised. They became the National Association Opposed to Woman Suffrage. This organization published *The Women's Protest* in 1912. The NAOWS disbanded in 1920 when the Nineteenth Amendment was passed.

Some men organized anti-suffrage groups, too, but mostly it was women's groups. The Men's Anti-Ratification League of Montgomery, Alabama, worked against having the Nineteenth Amendment ratified. There were no organized anti-suffragist societies in Canada. Some believe this is because the suffragist movement in Canada was considered to be more **conservative** than in the United States.

▼ Curious men examine material posted in the window of the National Association Opposed to Woman Suffrage's headquarters in 1911.

▼ Some of the anti-suffrage leaders who led a party of about 1,200 people up the Hudson River in New York State for an anti-suffrage event on May 13, 1913.

HISTORY REPEATED

". . . women have fought for everybody else's equal rights. It's our time to have wage equality once and for all and equal rights for women in the United States of America."

Actor Patricia Arquette during her Oscar acceptance speech for Best Supporting Actress, February 22, 2015

Even after women in North America had earned the right to vote, there was—and still is—more work to do toward gaining full equality between the sexes. Issues, such as **reproductive rights** and equal pay in the workforce, became the next major challenges for women.

A new wave of social reform began during the 1960s in North America. The civil rights movement and the **feminist movement**—also called the women's **liberation** movement—both fought for equality in terms of race and sex, respectively. Women's liberation groups fought for maternity benefits, affordable day-care services, and equality in the workplace, regardless of gender. In Canada, the average hourly wage of women working full time was only 87 percent of what men earned in 2011. In the United States in 2014, women, on average, made 78 cents for every dollar that a man earned. One reason for this **discrepancy** is that many women work at **menial** or lower-paying jobs, often because of their responsibility to the home and family.

Equality for women is an ongoing, global struggle. The Swedish website www.beaman.se asks the question: "What does a woman need to do to get a raise?" The answer is: "Be a man." This protest video is a primary source that informs the viewer about the inequalities in the workforce, while a woman is transformed by a professional makeup artist into appearing to be a man.

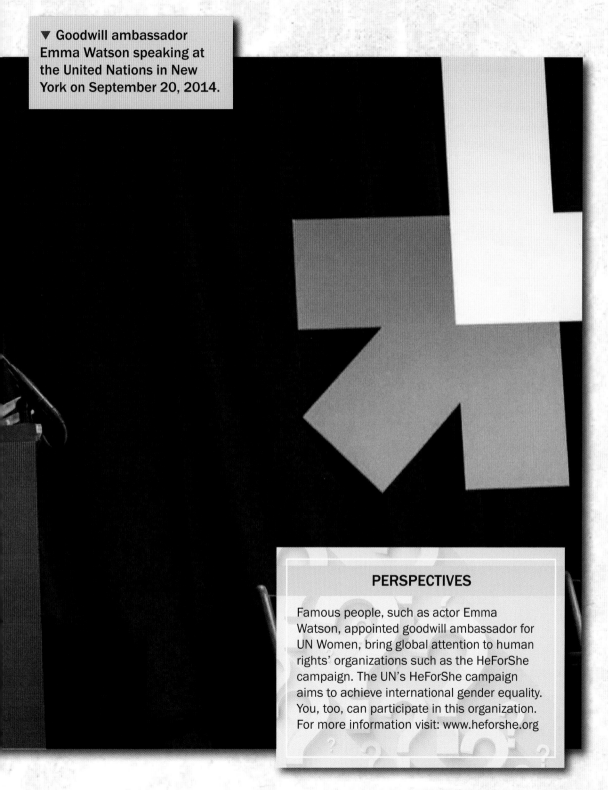

▼ Goodwill ambassador Emma Watson speaking at the United Nations in New York on September 20, 2014.

PERSPECTIVES

Famous people, such as actor Emma Watson, appointed goodwill ambassador for UN Women, bring global attention to human rights' organizations such as the HeForShe campaign. The UN's HeForShe campaign aims to achieve international gender equality. You, too, can participate in this organization. For more information visit: www.heforshe.org

VIOLENCE AGAINST WOMEN

The Declaration on the Elimination of Violence against Women defines violence against women as "any act of gender-based violence that results in . . . physical, sexual or psychological harm or suffering to women . . . whether occurring in public or in private life." Violence against women can happen in a woman's home, or in the community she lives in. It happens during war or peace. It happens in prisons, hospitals, parks, and cars. It is an international issue that occurs in every country. Historically, there were often no laws to protect women from violent acts. Although many countries have changed laws to protect women, violence against women still occurs.

PERSPECTIVES

Men and women have been fighting for human rights for more than 100 years. In 1993, the Women's Action Coalition conducted a march for women's rights. Betty Friedan is a famous feminist author who took part in the march. Betty Friedan's book *The Feminine Mystique*, published in 1963, inspired the women's rights movement throughout the 1960s.

EVIDENCE RECORD CARD

An excerpt from a speech given by UN Secretary-General Ban Ki-moon on November 25, 2014.
LEVEL Primary source
MATERIAL Videotaped speech given by UN Secretary-General Ban Ki-moon on the International Day for the Elimination of Violence against Women on November 25, 2014
LOCATION United Nations Headquarters, New York
DATE November 25, 2014
SOURCE United Nations

▲ Her Highness Princess Ameerah Al-Taweel of Saudi Arabia speaking at the Women Empowerment Group meeting in Dubai on the eve of International Woman's Day, March 10, 2012

In Canada, on December 6, 1989, a man named Marc Lépine entered a school called École Polytechnique de Montreal. Armed with a gun, he entered a classroom and separated men from women. He shot and killed fourteen women because he thought they were "feminists." He also stabbed and shot others who survived the attack, before committing suicide. In 1991, the Canadian government declared December 6 the National Day of Remembrance and Action on Violence against Women. The day was created so that Canadians would become more aware of this human rights issue in Canada. It also inspired the White Ribbon Campaign, a global organization of mostly men who work toward ending violence against women. On November 25—the UN's International Day for Elimination of Violence against Women—people are encouraged to wear a white ribbon to show their support. Organizations and special days such as these draw global attention to the inequalities between men and women that exist today.

"If we stand together in homes, communities, countries and internationally, we can challenge discrimination and [lack of punishment] and put a stop to practices and customs that encourage, ignore or tolerate the global disgrace of violence against women and girls."

UN Secretary-General Ban Ki-moon

▲ U.S. Secretary of State Hillary Rodham Clinton meets with women of the Upendo Women's Cooperative group in Mlandizi, Tanzania.

WORLDWIDE HUMAN RIGHTS

In some countries, women have only just recently gained suffrage. Women in Saudi Arabia were first enfranchised in 2015. In this conservative country, women have few basic rights and are allowed to own cars but not actually drive them. Saudi Arabian women's rights activists Manal al-Sharif and Wajeha al-Huwaider protested by filming and posting a video on YouTube showing al-Sharif driving a car. She was later arrested for doing so and imprisoned for a week. There is no actual government law against women driving, but only men are given driving licenses. In Saudi Arabia, it is a religious law that restricts women from driving.

ANALYZE THIS

This photograph was taken on October 12, 2014, to celebrate Malala Yousafzai winning the Nobel Peace Prize. Do you understand the words on the sign? What does this tell you about the global reaction and support for Malala?

◀ Activists in Surakarta in Indonesia celebrate the award of the Nobel Peace Prize to Malala Yousafzai in 2014.

"We know that we still have a long way to go for equality between men and women . . . to be a reality. . . . The structures that support women have been chronically underfunded and so has been the women's movement. As a result, too many women, especially in less-developed countries, have nothing to show for change as yet."

UN Women's Executive Director Phumzile Mlambo-Ngcuka, speaking on International Women's Day, March 8, 2015

In some countries, such as Pakistan, women are denied basic human rights such as education. In 2009, a girl named Malala Yousafzai wrote a blog about her life under the **Taliban** regime in Pakistan for the British Broadcasting Corporation (BBC). The Taliban believe that women should not be educated. Yousafzai became a popular activist for women's education in Pakistan and went on to make public speeches about girls' rights for education. In 2012, Taliban gunmen attacked a school bus and shot Yousafzai in the head, as well as two other girls. All three survived the attack. After her recovery, Yousafzai continued her activism for women's rights. In 2014, she became the youngest person to be awarded the Nobel Peace Price.

Even though great strides have been made in the last 100 years toward women's rights, much more work has yet to be done. Women around the world continue to fight for equality in human rights. International Women's Day is an annual celebration that raises global awareness of women's continuing struggle for human rights and equality. Some countries celebrate it as a national holiday and honor the women in their lives on that day.

▼ Slutwalk is an annual protest march that began in Toronto in 2011. It started in response to a police officer saying that, to avoid being sexually assaulted, women should not dress like sluts. Other countries have since organized their own Slutwalks.

TIMELINE

1790

1792 Feminist writer Mary Wollstonecraft publishes *A Vindication of the Rights of Woman*

1830s Women become active participants in social reform movements such as the temperance and abolition societies

1840 Abolition activists Elizabeth Cady Stanton and Lucretia Mott talk about forming a society to fight for women's rights, after being turned away at the World Anti-Slavery Convention in London, England

1848 Stanton and Mott organize the first American women's rights convention in Seneca Falls, New York

1851 Abolitionist and women's rights activist Sojourner Truth delivers her famous "Ain't I A Woman?" speech at the Women's Rights Convention held in Akron, Ohio

1861 The American Civil War begins

1865 The American Civil war ends, ending slavery for African Americans

1869 American women first gain their right to vote in Wyoming Territory

1869 Susan B. Anthony and Elizabeth Cady Stanton form the National Woman Suffrage Association (NWSA); Lucy Stone, her husband Henry Blackwell, and Julia Ward Howe form the American Woman Suffrage Association (AWSA)

1872 Anthony and other women try to vote during the U.S. presidential election; all are turned away at the polls or arrested

1877 Emily Howard Stowe founds Canada's first suffrage organization, known as the Toronto Women's Literary Guild

1878 The Woman Suffrage Amendment—also known as the Susan B. Anthony Amendment—is presented to Congress but is not passed

1883 Toronto Women's Literary Guild is renamed Canadian Women's Suffrage Association

1884 The National Council of Women in Canada is formed

1890 The NWSA and AWSA combine to become the National American Woman Suffrage Association (NAWSA)

1900

1900

1914 World War I begins; Canada   enters war

1917 The United States enters World War I; Canada passes the Wartime Elections Act that enfranchises Canadian women serving in the armed forces or with a male relative in the armed forces

1918 Some Canadian women federally enfranchised; U.S. House of Representatives passes Woman   Suffrage Amendment

1919 Congress approves Nineteenth Amendment

1920 August 26: Nineteenth Amendment   is ratified

1920 Dominion Elections Act enfranchises most Canadian women

1965 The United States passes Voting Rights Act; all Americans, regardless of race, are enfranchised

1960 All aboriginal Canadians are enfranchised

1965

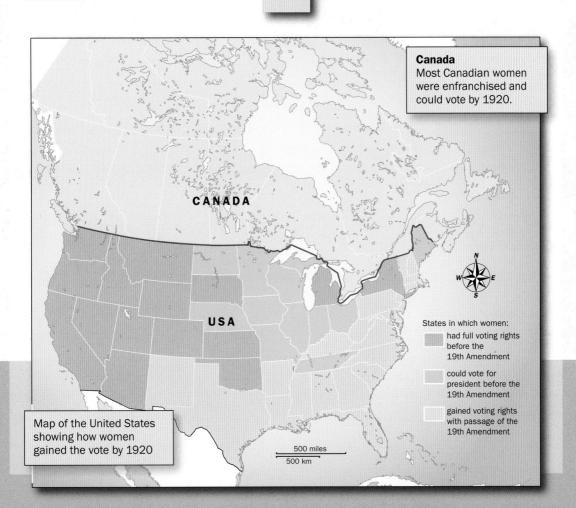

Canada
Most Canadian women were enfranchised and could vote by 1920.

Map of the United States showing how women gained the vote by 1920

States in which women:

had full voting rights before the 19th Amendment

could vote for president before the 19th Amendment

gained voting rights with passage of the 19th Amendment

500 miles
500 km

BIBLIOGRAPHY

QUOTATIONS

p.4 Nellie McClung:
www.uppercanadahistory.ca/foreword.html

p.6 Aristotle. *Politics*. Trans. Benjamin Jowett:
http://classics.mit.edu/Aristotle/politics.1.one.html

p.8 Wollstonecraft, Mary. *A Vindication of the Rights of Woman*:
www.gutenberg.org/ebooks/3420

p.11 Lyrics from "We'll Show You When We Come to Vote:" www.pdmusic.org/1800s/68wvattm.txt

p.13 From "Women Together," taken from *The Public Ledger and Daily Transcript*, reprinted in HWS 1 (*History of Woman Suffrage*, Vol. 1), p.805: www.gutenberg.org/files/28020/28020-h.htm#CHAPTER_IV

p.14 *James and Lucretia Mott: Life and Letters*. Ed. Anna Davis Hallowell, Houghton, Mifflin, 1890. p.113.

p.16 *The Militant Husbandette*, 1913:
www.iowaheritage.org/items/show/68499

pp.18–19 Excerpts from Sojourner Truth's "Ain't I A Woman?" speech: www.nolo.com/legal-encyclopedia/content/truth-woman-speech.html

p.20 Ossoli, Margaret Fuller. *Woman in the Nineteenth Century*. 1845. Chapter: The Wrongs and Duties of American Women:
www.gutenberg.org/files/8642/8642-h/8642-h.htm#poverty

p.23 Excerpt from the Declaration of Sentiments:
www.womensrightsfriends.org/pdfs/1848_declaration_of_sentiments.pdf

p.25 Excerpt from the "Declaration of Rights of the Women of the United States:"
www.lib.rochester.edu/index.cfm?PAGE=2941

p.26 U.S. President Woodrow Wilson's appeal to the Senate, September 30, 1918

p.29 Quote found at:
www.famous5.ca/index.php/the-famous-5-women/the-famous-5-women#henrietta-muir-edwards

p.30 Elizabeth Cady Stanton, speaking at the NAWSA convention, February 12–18, 1902

p.32 Quote from:
http://womhist.alexanderstreet.com/colosuff/doc19.htm

p.34 Household hints pamphlet, published by the National Association Opposed to Woman Suffrage, in 1910:
http://cdn.theatlantic.com/static/mt/assets/hua_hsu/barkhorn_womenvoters2.jpg

p.36 Patricia Arquette's speech:
www.youtube.com/watch?v=w7JZCsSD92E

p.39 Excerpt from UN Secretary-General Ban Ki-moon's Message for 2014 on the International Day for the Elimination of Violence against Women, found at:
www.un.org/en/events/endviolenceday/2014/sgmessage.shtml

p.40 Phumzile Mlambo-Ngcuka's speech:
www.internationalwomensday.com/resources.asp#.VP7tGiiRm-I

INTERNET GUIDELINES

Finding good source material on the Internet can sometimes be a challenge. Analyze each site you find and check out the information on it. How reliable is it?

- Who writes and/or sponsors the page? Is it an expert in the field, a person who experienced the event, or just a person with a strong opinion?
- Is the site well known and up to date? Government and college websites often have lots of easy-to-find sources and information.
- Can you verify the facts with another source? Always double-check by comparing the information on several websites.

- Did you determine whether what you find is a primary or secondary source? Do your secondary sources seem to be based on a variety of primary sources?
- Have you kept a list of the websites you've visited? This can help you verify information later.

TO FIND OUT MORE

Non-Fiction

Anderson, Jennifer Joline. *Women's Rights Movement* (Essential Library of Social Change). ABDO, 2014.

Benoit, Peter. *Women's Right to Vote* (Cornerstones of Freedom). Children's Press, 2014.

Cooper, Ilene. *A Woman in the House (and Senate)*. Abrams Books, 2014.

Isecke, Harriet. *Women's Suffrage: Fighting for Women's Rights.* Teacher Created Materials, 2011.

Nardo, Don. *The Women's Movement* (World History). Lucent Books, 2011.

Yousafzai, Malala. *I Am Malala: How One Girl Stood Up for Education and Changed the World*. Little, Brown, 2014.

Fiction

Ellis, Deborah. *My Name is Parvana*. Groundwood Books, 2012.

Winters, Cat. *The Cure for Dreaming*. Amulet Books, 2014.

WEBSITES AND MULTIMEDIA

Library of Congress

Website resource for primary source documents on Women's Rights (and other historical subjects): www.loc.gov

America's Story from America's Library

A website resource for history and biographies: www.americaslibrary.gov

National Women's History Museum

A website that provides history and primary sources documenting women's contributions and accomplishments in the United States: www.nwhm.org

Parliament of Canada

Government website that gives history of women's vote in Canada: www.parl.gc.ca

The Nellie Clung Foundation Website

Good resource for history of Canadian women's suffrage: www.ournellie.com

Emma Watson

Listen to Emma Watson's HeForShe 2014 campaign speech: www.youtube.com/watch?v=gkjW9PZBRfk

GLOSSARY

abolitionist Person who wants to end a practice such as slavery

aboriginal A person whose ancestors were the original inhabitants of a country

activist A person who takes action toward change

African American American whose ancestors came from Africa

age A distinct period of history

alien-born Born in a country other than the country one is living in

amendment Change to the meaning or words of a law or constitution

analyze To study closely and determine how the evidence fits together

artifacts Objects made by human beings

ballot An official paper on which to vote in an election

bias Prejudice in favor of or against one thing, person, or group

black Another term for African Americans

blog A website or web page in which its owner records personal opinions on a regular basis and provides useful links to other sites

century A period of 100 years

chivalrous Describing behaving according to the cultural beliefs and manners in which a man was expected to treat a woman

coined Invented or made up

conservative Acting or approaching a situation with more caution than most would use

constitution Written laws and principles by which a country is governed

context The setting—the time and place—in which an event occurs; context includes the social customs and culture that shape the generation of people who live during that era

convention A conference or meeting of members of a society called together to discuss an important issue

corrupt Make less pure

credible Something that can be believed

culture The ideas, customs, and behavior of a people

decade A period of ten years

discrepancy A difference between things that should be the same

disenfranchise To remove someone's right to vote

document A piece of paper that provides an official record of something

eloquence The ability to speak clearly and understandably

emancipate To free a person from another person's control

enfranchise To allow a person to vote

era A long period of history, with a distinct characteristic

evidence The body of facts, clues or information to show whether something is true

eyewitness A person present at an event and who can report it at a later date

fair sex An old-fashioned term used for a person of the female gender or sex; the word "fair" was associated with beauty

feminist A person who believes that men and women should have equal rights

feminist movement An organized campaign, usually led by women, to get equal rights for all people, regardless of sex

First Nation A term used to describe some of the aboriginal people living in Canada, although it does not include the Inuit, who are also aboriginal

generation All the people born and living at the same time

heist An armed robbery, often of a bank

herstory The documentation of the past from a female perspective

historian A person who studies history

history Past events and their description

hunger strike Protesting an action by refusing to eat

husbandette An insulting term used to describe a weak man whose wife was a suffragette

Indian status A legal identity law for aboriginal persons in Canada

inequality A lack of equality or equal status with other people

infer To form an idea or opinion based on given evidence

interpret Explain the meaning of something

liberate To set free

lithography A printing process from which an image is produced from a flat stone surface that has been prepared with lithographic ink

media Plural of medium; medium is one way of expressing an idea

menial A low-paying job that does not require special education or skill

millennium A period of 1,000 years

municipal The local government of an area such as a town or city

online Live and connected to a computer

picket To protest by standing or marching while holding a sign that shows what a person is protesting against

primary source A first-hand account or direct evidence of an event

provincial government The government of a province in Canada

quarterly Something that is done every three months, or four times within a year

quotation Words that are quoted, or repeated or rewritten, from another source

ratify To confirm something such as an amendment or change to a constitution

reform To change something to improve it

reliable Someone or something that can be depended upon

repercussion A negative consequence from an earlier action

reproductive rights The freedoms and rights related to reproduction or childbearing, and reproductive health

score The printed notes and words of a musical composition

secondary source Material created by studying primary sources

slave A person owned by another and treated as property, without any rights

social standards The commonly accepted rules of behavior in a society

sourcing Asking questions about a primary source

stenographer A person trained and skilled at writing or typing notes in shorthand, or abbreviations and symbols

suffrage The right to vote

suffragette A suffragist prepared to use militant tactics to achieve the vote

suffragist A person who believes that another person (especially of the female gender) should be allowed to vote

Taliban A militant Islamic group that often controls populations through violence

temperance Not drinking alcohol

utensil An object for use in the kitchen or home

vote The right to cast a ballot to elect someone to public office or to decide on an important change to the law or constitution

INDEX